Top 100 Recipes
Milkshakes & Smoothie

Copyright © 2020 Alexey Evdokimov. All Rights Reserved

Published by Alexey Evdokimov

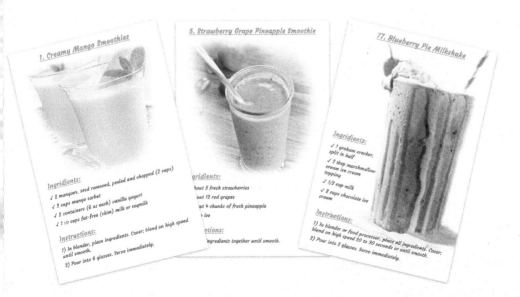

1. Creamy Mango Smoothies

Ingridients:

√ 2 mangoes, seed removed, peeled and chopped (2 cups)

√ 2 cups mango sorbet

√ 2 containers (6 oz each) vanilla yogurt

√ 1 1/2 cups fat-free (skim) milk or soymilk

Instructions:

1) In blender, place ingredients. Cover; blend on high speed until smooth.

2) Pour into 6 glasses. Serve immediately.

5. Strawberry Grape Pineapple Smoothie

Ingridients:

...bout 5 fresh strawberries

...out 12 red grapes

...ut 4 chunks of fresh pineapple

... ice

...tions:

...ngredients together until smooth.

77. Blueberry Pie Milkshake

Ingridients:

√ 1 graham cracker, split in half

√ 2 tbsp marshmallow cream ice cream topping

√ 1/2 cup milk

√ 2 cups chocolate ice cream

Instructions:

1) In blender or food processor, place all ingredients. Cover; blend on high speed 20 to 30 seconds or until smooth.

2) Pour into 2 glasses. Serve immediately.

Table of Contents:

Milkshake Recipes:

History Milkshake and Smoothie

The term milkshake was first used, in print, in 1885. Milkshakes were an alcoholic whiskey drink that has been described as a "...sturdy, healthful eggnog type of drink, with eggs, whiskey, etc., served as a tonic as well as a treat".

By 1900, the term milkshake referred to "wholesome drinks made with chocolate, strawberry, or vanilla syrups".

The milkshake made it into the mainstream when in 1922 a Walgreens employee in Chicago, Ivar "Pop" Coulson, took an old-fashioned malted milk (milk, chocolate, and malt) and added two scoops of ice cream, creating a drink which became popular at a surprising rate, soon becoming a high-demand drink for young adults around the country.

By the 1930s, milkshakes were a popular drink at malt shops. The automation of milkshakes developed in the 1930s, after the invention of freon-cooled refrigerators provided a safe, reliable way of automatically making and dispensing ice cream.

In the late 1930s, several newspaper articles show that the term "frosted" was used to refer to milkshakes made with ice cream.

In the 1950s, a milkshake machine salesman named Ray Kroc bought exclusive rights to a milkshake maker from inventor Earl Prince, and went on to use automated milkshake machines to speed up production in a major fast-food chain.

In 2000 there was developed a reduced-sugar, low-fat milk shakes for school lunch programs. The shakes have half the sugar and only 10% of the fat of commercial fast-food shakes.

In the 2000s, milkshakes began being used as part of the new trend of boutique-style "spa dentistry," which aim to relax dental patients and reduce their anxiety.

Nowadays we are lucky that we can a good milkshake. Just like the smoothie there are a countless number of flavors when it comes to milkshakes.

Smoothie

A smoothie (alternatively spelled smoothy, the name comes from the smooth property of the emulsion) is a blended and sometimes sweetened beverage made from fresh fruit (fruit smoothie) and in special cases can contain chocolate or peanut butter. In addition to fruit, many smoothies include crushed ice, frozen fruit, honey or contain syrup and ice ingredients. They have a milkshake-like consistency that is thicker than slush drinks. They can also contain milk, yogurt or ice cream.

Smoothies are often marketed to health-conscious people, and some restaurants offer add-ins such as soy milk, whey powder, green tea, herbal supplements, or nutritional supplement mixes.

One of the first Machine for mixing beverages

Smoothies became widely available in the United States in the late 1960s when ice cream vendors and health food stores began selling them. By the 1990s and 2000s, smoothies became available at mainstream cafés and coffee shops and in pre-bottled versions at supermarkets all over the world.

Measurement Conversion Chart

WEIGHT

1 oz = 28.35 g
1 g = 0.035 oz
1 kg = 35 oz (2.2 Lbs)

MPERIAL	IMETRIC
1/2 oz	15 g
1 oz	30 g
2 oz	60 g
3 oz	90 g
4 oz	110 g
5 oz	140 g
6 oz	170 g
7 oz	200 g
8 oz	225 g
9 oz	255 g
10 oz	280 g
11 oz	310 g
12 oz	340 g
13 oz	370 g
14 oz	400 g
15 oz	425 g
1 lb	450 g

LIQUID

1 cup (US) = 250 ml
1 fl oz = 29.5 ml
1 ml = 0.34 fl oz

METRIC	PINT	CUPS	FL OZ.
15 ml		1 tbsp	½
30 ml		⅛	1
60 ml		¼	2
75 ml		⅓	2 ½
100 ml			3 ½
125 ml		½	4 ½
150 ml	¼		5
180 ml		¾	6
200 ml			7
250 ml		1	8
275 ml	½		10
300 ml			11
400 ml			14
500 ml		2	18
570 ml	1		20
750 ml		3	26
1.0 l	1¾	4	35

Glass Types for Cocktails and Smoothies

Hurricane Glass
for Tropical Cocktails
400-480 mL

Poco Grande
for Frozen Cocktails
250-400 mL

Collins
for Large Cocktails
with Ice and Soda
240-320 mL

Highball
for Long Cocktails you
Drink Slowly
160-240 mL

Fountain Glass
for Soda, Milkshakes
and Smoothie
200-500 mL

TIKI
for Milkshakes and Tropical Cocktails
200-700 mL

Smoothie Jar
or Milkshakes, Smoothies
and Summer Lemonades
250-1000 mL

Jar with Handle
for Milkshakes, Smoothies
and Cream Shakes
200-750 mL

Plastic Container
for Cocktails, Desserts
and Drinks
250-600 mL

Cocktail Bottle
for Milk Cocktails and
Smoothies
250-800 mL

Tumbler
for Juices, Water
and Large Cocktails
200-320 mL

Irish Coffee Glass
for Hot and Coffee Drinks
and Tea Cocktails
240-280 mL

1. Creamy Mango Smoothies

Ingridients:

✓ 2 mangoes, seed removed, peeled and chopped (2 cups)

✓ 2 cups mango sorbet

✓ 2 containers (6 oz each) vanilla yogurt

✓ 1 1/2 cups fat-free (skim) milk or soymilk

Instructions:

1) In blender, place ingredients. Cover; blend on high speed until smooth.

2) Pour into 6 glasses. Serve immediately.

2. Blueberry Smoothies

Ingridients:

✓ 1 cup organic blueberries (from 8-oz bag)

✓ 1/2 cup vanilla soymilk or fat-free (skim) milk

✓ 1 container (6 oz) lemon burst or French vanilla yogurt

✓ Honey, if desired

Instructions:

1) In blender, place blueberries, soymilk and yogurt. Cover; blend on high speed about 1 minute or until smooth. Sweeten to taste with honey.

2) Pour into 2 glasses. Serve immediately.

3. Stoplight Smoothie "Flight"

Ingridients:

✓ 3 kiwis peeled and chopped

✓ 1 cup chopped strawberries

✓ 2 bananas, peeled and chopped

✓ 1 1/2 cups vanilla-flavored Light yogurt

✓ 1 1/2 cups milk

✓ 6 Tbsp honey

✓ 3 cups ice

✓ Food red, green and yellow coloring (optional)

Instructions:

1) Place peeled and chopped kiwi, 1/2 cup yogurt, 1/2 cup milk, 2 tsp honey and 1 cup ice in a blender. Blend until smooth. Pour equally into three 1-cup glasses and top with whipped cream, if desired.

2) Repeat step 1 with the strawberry and banana flavored smoothies.

3) Set in a row like a stoplight and serve!

4) Optional: For brighter colors, add a few drops of food coloring (green to kiwi, red to strawberry, etc.) to the blender before blending.

4. Chilling Jack-O'-Lantern Smoothies

Ingridients:

✓ 1 tablespoon semisweet chocolate chips

✓ 4 plastic cups (8 to 9 oz each)

✓ 3 containers (6 oz) orange crème or harvest peach yogurt

✓ 1/4 cup frozen (thawed) orange juice concentrate

✓ 1 can (11 oz) mandarin orange segments, chilled, drained

✓ 1 banana, sliced

Instructions:

1) In small microwavable bowl, melt chocolate chips on High for 1 minute or until melted. With tip of knife, spread chocolate on inside of each plastic cup to resemble eyes, nose and mouth of jack-o'-lantern. Repeat with 3 more cups. Refrigerate 5 minutes or until chocolate is set.

2) Meanwhile, in blender container, place all remaining ingredients; cover and blend until smooth. Pour into chocolate painted cups.

5. Strawberry Grape Pineapple Smoothie

Ingridients:

✓ About 5 fresh strawberries

✓ About 12 red grapes

✓ About 4 chunks of fresh pineapple

✓ 1 cup ice

Instructions:

1) Blend ingredients together until smooth.

6. Green Smoothie

Ingridients:

✓ 2 cups fresh baby spinach, rinsed

✓ 1 Granny Smith green apple, cored

✓ 1 banana, peeled

✓ 1 orange, peeled

✓ 1 tsp. grated fresh ginger (or 1/2 tsp. ground ginger)

Instructions:

1) Combine all ingredients in a blender and mix until smooth and well-combined.

7. Pineapple Ginger Smoothie

Ingridients:

✓ 1 1/2 cups diced fresh pineapple

✓ 1 banana

✓ 1/2 cup greek yogurt (I used vanilla, but you can choose your favorite flavor)

✓ 1 Tbsp. grated fresh ginger

✓ 1/2 cup ice

✓ 1/2 cup pineapple juice or water

Instructions:

1) Blend all ingredients together in a blender until smooth. Serve immediately.

8. Fresh Orange Smoothie

Ingridients:

√ 4 fresh oranges, peeled

√ 2 cups ice

√ 1/3 cup milk (your preference - regular, soy, coconut, etc.)

√ 2 Tbsp. honey (or agave nectar, or sugar) - optional

√ 1 tsp. vanilla

√ Zest of 1 orange

Instructions:

1) Combine all ingredients in a blender, and blend until smooth. Add more ice if you would like.

9. Frozen Banana-Coconut Refresher

Ingridients:

✓ 1/3 cup fresh lime juice

✓ 3 bananas, peeled and broken into pieces

✓ 1/4 cup granulated sugar

✓ 1/3 cup coconut milk

✓ 2 cups ice cubes

✓ 1 lime, cut into 4 wedges

Instructions:

1) Place all of the ingredients, except for the lime wedges, in a blender and puree until smooth.

2) Pour into 4 martini glasses, garnish with a lime wedge, and serve.

10. Cherry Smoothie

Ingridients:

✓ 1/2 cup non-fat milk

✓ 1/2 cup greek yogurt, plain or vanilla

✓ 1 cup cherries, frozen

✓ 1 tsp vanilla extract

✓ 1/2 tsp stevia or more to taste

Instructions:

1) Place all ingredients in a blender and process until smooth.

2) Serve with reduced fat whip cream and a cherry!

11. Coconut Mango Smoothie

Ingridients:

✓ 1 cup chopped mango

✓ 1 banana, sliced and frozen

✓ 1/2 cup coconut milk

✓ 1/2 cup water

✓ A handful of ice cubes

✓ 1/2 teaspoon lime zest

✓ 1 sweetener packet, or 1/2 teaspoon sugar

✓ 1/2 teaspoon coconut extract

Instructions:

1) Combine all ingredients in a blender.

2) Blend on high until smooth and creamy.

12. Chocolate Banana Cookies & Cream Smoothies

Ingridients:

√ 1 cup fat-free (skim) milk

√ 4 creme-filled chocolate sandwich cookies

√ 1 pouch (7.6 oz) Yoplait Smoothie chocolate banana

√ Whipped cream topping in aerosol can, if desired

Instructions:

1) In blender, place milk, cookies and contents of smoothie pouch. Cover; blend on high speed 1 minute to 1 minute 30 seconds, stopping to scrape sides as necessary, until smooth.

2) Pour into 2 glasses. Top with whipped topping. Serve immediately.

13. I Heart You Fresh Strawberry Smoothie

Ingridients:

✓ 1 cup vanilla soy milk (almond milk works well too)

✓ 1/2 cup strawberry soy yogurt

✓ 1 small ripe banana

✓ 1/2 cup ice cubes

✓ 1 1/4 cups mixed frozen berries (raspberries, strawberries, blueberries)

✓ 3-4 fresh strawberries

✓ 2 Tbsp agave or maple syrup

Instructions:

1) Gather all your ingredients.

2) Add the milk, frozen fruit, banana, ice, yogurt and sweetener to you blender. Blend until smooth. Thickness tastes vary. I like my smoothies thick, my husband likes them thin. Add more milk if the blend is too stiff. Add more ice/fruit if it is too thin.

3) Lastly, pulse in the fresh strawberries – I like to add the tender fresh fruit last so I don't mush it up too much.

4) Serve in smoothie glasses, garnish with a fresh strawberry on the glass. Pink straws optional, but recommended!

14. Blueberry Watermelon Smoothie

Ingridients:

✓ 3 cups blueberries

✓ 3 cups cubed watermelon

✓ 1 ½ cups ice

Instructions:

1) Add blueberries and watermelon to the container of a blender. Blend on high for about 40 seconds or until completely pureed. Then, stop blender and remove the lid. Add ice to the puree and secure the lid back onto the container. Turn the blender on high for 40 more seconds or until completely blended and smooth with no ice pieces remaining.

2) Serve immediately.

15. Berry Burst Banana Smoothies

Ingridients:

√ 2 (6-oz.) containers Fat-Free Strawberry, Mixed Berry or Red Raspberry Yogurt

√ 1 1/2 cups Berry Burst Cheerios triple berry cereal

√ 1 cup fresh strawberry halves or raspberries, or Cascadian Farm frozen organic strawberries

√ 1 cup milk

√ 1 banana, sliced

√ Berry Burst Cheerios triple berry cereal

Instructions:

1) In blender container, combine all ingredients. Cover; blend at high speed for 10 seconds.

2) Stop blender and uncover; scrape down sides of container. Cover; blend an additional 20 seconds or until smooth.

3) Pour yogurt mixture into 2 glasses. Serve immediately.

16. Hurricane Smoothie

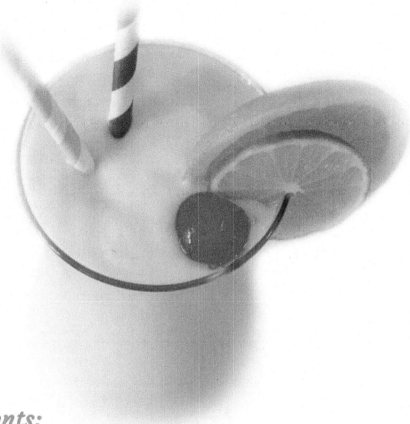

Ingridients:

✓ 1 cup pineapple, frozen

✓ 1/2 cup orange juice

✓ 1 tsp lime juice

✓ 1/2 cup greek yogurt, plain

✓ 1/8 tsp rum extract

✓ 1/4 tsp stevia (to taste)

Instructions:

1) Place all ingredients in a blender and process until smooth.

17. Melon-Raspberry Smoothies

Ingridients:

- ✓ 1 cup cubed cantaloupe or honeydew melon
- ✓ 1 cup fresh raspberries
- ✓ 1 container 6 oz strawberry mango yogurt
- ✓ 2 tablespoons milk
- ✓ 1 tablespoon sugar

Instructions:

1) In blender, place ingredients. Cover; blend on high speed 20 to 30 seconds or until smooth.

2) Pour into 2 glasses. Serve immediately.

18. Green Tea Smoothie

Ingridients:

√ 2 Cups Green Tea, strongly brewed and frozen

√ 1/3 Cup Mountain High Yoghurt

√ 1/2 Cup Almond Milk

√ 1 Cup Honeydew Melon

√ 2 Tablespoons Honey

Instructions:

1) Steep 2 cups of boiling water with two green tea bags. Let sit for 10-15 minutes to make sure tea is very strong.

2) Pour tea into ice cube trays to freeze. Let freeze solid.

3) Add green tea ice cubes to blender with other ingredients.

4) Blend until smooth and serve immediately.

19. Fiber One Strawberry Smoothies

Ingridients:

✓ 1 container 6 oz strawberry yogurt

✓ 1 cup fresh strawberry halves or frozen unsweetened whole strawberries

✓ 3/4 cup fat-free (skim) milk

✓ 2 tablespoons original bran cereal

Instructions:

1) In blender, place all ingredients. Cover; blend on high speed 10 seconds.

2) Scrape down sides of blender. Cover; blend about 20 seconds longer or until smooth.

3) Pour into 2 glasses. Serve immediately.

20. Super Spinach Smoothie

Ingridients:

✓ 1 cup fat-free (skim) milk

✓ 1 (7.6 oz) package frozen smoothie triple berry

✓ 1/2 cup torn fresh spinach

Instructions:

1) In blender container, place milk, contents of Yoplait Frozen Smoothie bag and spinach. Cover; blend on high speed 1 minute to 1 minute 30 seconds, stopping blender to scrape down sides as necessary, until smooth. Pour into glasses.

21. Super Athlete Spinach Smoothies

Ingridients:

✓ 1 box (9 oz) green frozen chopped spinach

✓ 1 container (6 oz) greek blueberry yogurt

✓ 1 avocado half, pitted and peeled

✓ 3/4 cup cranberry-blueberry juice

✓ 1/2 cup frozen organic blueberries

Instructions:

1) Microwave spinach as directed on box. Rinse with cold water until cooled. Drain, squeezing out as much liquid as possible.

2) In blender, place 1/4 cup of the cooked spinach and remaining ingredients. (Cover and refrigerate remaining spinach for another use.) Cover; blend on high speed about 30 seconds or until smooth.

3) Pour into 2 glasses. Serve immediately.

22. Chocolate Banana Cashew Smoothie

Ingridients:

√ 3 oz. nonfat vanilla greek yogurt

√ 1/2 frozen banana

√ 1/4 avocado

√ 1/2 cup spinach

√ 1/2 cup chocolate soy milk

√ 1/8 cup raw cashews

√ 1/2 cup water

For garnish:

√ 3 dark chocolate chips

Instructions:

1) Add ingredients to a blender (save three cashews for topping) and mix until smooth.

2) Pour into a glass.

3) Chop remaining cashews and chocolate chips, sprinkle on the top, and enjoy.

23. Strawberry-Banana Smoothies

Ingridients:

√ 1 1/2 cups vanilla soymilk

√ 1 bag 10 oz frozen organic unsweetened strawberries, partially thawed

√ 1 medium banana, cut into chunks

√ 1/3 cup calcium-enriched orange juice

√ Honey, if desired

Instructions:

1) In blender or food processor, place soymilk, strawberries, banana and orange juice. Cover; blend on high speed about 1 minute or until smooth. Sweeten to taste with honey.

2) Pour into 2 glasses. Serve immediately.

24. Apple-Kiwi Smoothie

Ingridients:

√ 1 small apple, peeled, cut into chunks

√ 1 kiwifruit, peeled, cut into chunks

√ 4 medium fresh strawberries

√ 2/3 cup creamy strawberry yogurt (from 2-lb container)

√ 1/3 cup apple juice

Instructions:

1) In blender, place ingredients. Cover; blend on high speed about 30 seconds or until smooth.

2) Pour into 2 glasses. Serve immediately.

25. Classic Strawberry Banana Smoothie

Ingridients:

✓ About 12 red grapes

✓ About 5 fresh strawberries

✓ 1/2 ripe banana

✓ 1/4 cup Greek yogurt

✓ 1 tablespoon honey

Instructions:

1) Add ingredients to blender in the order as listed in ingredients list. Blend on high for approximately 1 minute until creamy and smooth. Serve immediately.

26. Candy Corn Smoothies

Ingridients:

✓ 1 pint (2 cups) coconut sorbet, slightly softened

✓ 6 tablespoons milk

✓ 1 pint (2 cups) orange sherbet, slightly softened

✓ 1 pint (2 cups) lemon sorbet, slightly softened

✓ 4 drops yellow food color

✓ Candy corn, if desired

Instructions:

1) In blender, place coconut sorbet and 2 tablespoons of the milk. Cover; blend on high speed 30 to 60 seconds or until smooth. Divide evenly among 8 glasses. Place glasses in freezer.

2) Rinse blender. In blender, place orange sherbet and 2 tablespoons milk. Cover; blend on high speed 30 to 60 seconds or until smooth. Pour over coconut mixture in glasses, dividing evenly. Return glasses to freezer.

3) Rinse blender. In blender, place lemon sorbet, yellow food color and remaining 2 tablespoons milk. Cover; blend on high speed 30 to 60 seconds or until smooth. Pour over orange mixture in glasses, dividing evenly. Garnish with candy corn. Serve or freeze until serving time.

27. Lactose Free Peach-Mango Lassi

Ingridients:

√ 1 cup ice

√ 1 1/2 cups chopped mango

√ 1 cup original-flavored soymilk

√ 2 containers (6 oz each) peach yogurt

√ Ground ginger

Instructions:

1) In blender, place all ingredients except ginger. Cover; blend on medium speed about 2 minutes or until smooth.

2) Pour into 4 glasses; top with ginger. Serve immediately.

28. Taste-Of-The-Tropics Smoothies

Ingridients:

√ 1 cup light coconut milk

√ 1 bag (7.6 oz) frozen smoothie strawberry mango pineapple

√ 1/8 teaspoon ground ginger

Instructions:

1) In blender, place coconut milk, contents of Yoplait Frozen Smoothie bag and ginger. Cover; blend on high speed 1 minute to 1 minute 30 seconds, stopping blender to scrape down sides as necessary, until smooth. Pour into glasses.

29. Creamy Peach Smoothies

Ingridients:

✓ 1 cup frozen organic sliced peaches (from 10-oz bag)

✓ 1 container (6 oz) vanilla yogurt

✓ 3/4 cup orange juice

✓1 tablespoon honey

Instructions:

1) In blender or food processor, place all ingredients. Cover; blend on high speed about 1 minute or until smooth.

2) Pour into 2 glasses. Serve immediately.

30. Chocolate-Raspberry Smoothies

Ingridients:

✓ 2 cups light chocolate soymilk

✓ 1 cup frozen organic raspberries

✓ 1/2 teaspoon vanilla

Instructions:

1) Place all ingredients in blender or food processor. Cover; blend on low speed about 30 seconds or until smooth.

2) Pour into 2 glasses. Serve immediately.

31. Super Strawberry Smoothies

Ingridients:

✓ 1 bag (12 oz) frozen broccoli cuts

✓ 1 container (6 oz) vanilla yogurt

✓ 1 avocado half, pitted and peeled

✓ 3/4 cup pomegranate juice

✓ 1 cup frozen organic strawberries

Instructions:

1) Cook broccoli as directed on bag. Rinse with cold water until cooled. Drain well.

2) In blender, place 1/4 cup of the cooked broccoli and remaining ingredients. (Cover and refrigerate remaining broccoli for another use.) Cover; blend on high speed about 30 seconds or until smooth.

3) Pour into 2 glasses. Serve immediately.

32. Summer's Bounty Smoothies

Ingridients:

✓ 1 ripe banana, peeled, cut into chunks

✓ 1 ripe nectarine, peeled, pitted and quartered

✓ 4 to 5 large fresh strawberries, cut in half

✓ 1 cup strawberry frozen yogurt

Instructions:

1) In blender or food processor, place all ingredients. Cover; blend on high speed 20 to 30 seconds or until smooth.

2) Pour into 2 glasses. Serve immediately.

33. Peachy White Tea Smoothies

Ingridients:

✓ 2 cups soymilk

✓ 8 bags peach-flavored white tea

✓ 3 cups frozen sliced peaches

✓ 1/4 cup honey

Instructions:

1) In 1-quart saucepan, heat soymilk just to boiling over medium-high heat, stirring constantly; remove from heat. Add tea bags and push into soymilk; let stand 5 minutes. Discard teabags. Place saucepan with soymilk mixture in freezer 15 to 20 minutes to chill.

2) Place chilled soymilk, peaches and honey in blender or food processor. Cover; blend on high speed about 1 minute or until smooth. Pour into 2 glasses. Serve immediately.

34. Strawberry Kix Layered Smoothie

Ingridients:

✓ 2 containers strawberry yogurt

✓ 1 cup sliced fresh or frozen strawberries (no need to thaw)

✓ 1/2 cup orange juice

✓ 1 cup ice cubes

✓ 1 cup Kix cereal

Instructions:

1) In blender, place yogurt, strawberries and orange juice. Cover; blend on medium speed until smooth.

2) In 2 glasses, pour half of mixture. Add 1/2 cup cereal to each. Top with remaining mixture. Serve immediately.

35. Berry-Banana Smoothie

Ingridients:

✓ 1 cup vanilla, plain, strawberry or raspberry fat-free yogurt

✓ 1/2 cup round oat cereal

✓ 2 tablespoons ground flaxseed or flaxseed meal

✓ 1/2 cup fresh strawberry halves or raspberries, or frozen whole strawberries

✓ 1/2 cup fat-free (skim) milk

✓ 1 to 2 tablespoons sugar

✓ 1/2 banana

Instructions:

1) Place all ingredients in blender. Cover and blend on high speed 10 seconds; stop blender to scrape sides. Cover and blend about 20 seconds longer or until smooth.

2) Pour mixture into glasses. Serve immediately.

36. Broccoli Banana Blueberry Smoothies

Ingridients:

✓ 1/2 cup green giant frozen broccoli cuts

✓ 1 cup fat-free (skim) milk

✓ 1/2 medium banana

✓ 1 pouch (7.6 oz) smoothie blueberry pomegranate

Instructions:

1) Cook broccoli as directed on package; rinse with cold water. Drain.

2) In blender, place all ingredients. Cover; blend on high speed 1 minute to 1 minute 30 seconds, stopping to scrape sides as necessary, until smooth. Pour into 2 glasses. Serve immediately.

37. Berry Orange Smoothies

Ingridients:

✓ 1 cup fat-free (skim) milk

✓ 1 cup ready-to-eat baby-cut carrots

✓ 1 orange or 2 clementines, peeled and quartered

✓ 1 pouch (7.6 oz) smoothie triple berry

Instructions:

1) In blender, place all ingredients. Cover; blend on high speed 1 minute to 1 minute 30 seconds, stopping to scrape sides as necessary, until smooth.

2) Pour into 2 glasses. Serve immediately.

38. Triple Berry Spa Smoothies

Ingridients:

√ 1 cup fat-free (skim) milk

√ 3/4 cup cubed sliced cucumber

√ 1/2 avocado, pitted, peeled

√ 1 pouch (7.6 oz) smoothie triple berry

Instructions:

1) In blender, place all ingredients. Cover; blend on high speed 1 minute to 1 minute 30 seconds, stopping to scrape sides as necessary, until smooth.

2) Pour into 2 glasses. Serve immediately.

39. Greek Honey Oat Smoothies

Ingridients:

✓ 3/4 cup fat-free (skim) milk

✓ 1 container (6 oz) greek honey vanilla yogurt

✓ 2 oats 'n honey crunchy granola bars (1 pouch from 8.9-oz box), coarsely crushed

✓ 2 tablespoons honey

✓ 1 pouch (4.5 oz) smoothie greek mixed berry

Instructions:

1) In blender, place all ingredients. Cover; blend on high speed 1 minute to 1 minute 30 seconds, stopping to scrape sides as necessary, until smooth.

2) Pour into 2 glasses. Serve immediately.

40. Chocolate Hazelnut Breakfast Smoothies

Ingridients:

✓ 1 cup fat-free (skim) milk

✓ 1/2 cup chocolate cereal

✓ 3 tablespoons hazelnut spread with cocoa

✓ 1 pouch (7.6 oz) smoothie chocolate banana

Instructions:

1) In blender, place all ingredients. Cover; blend on high speed 1 minute to 1 minute 30 seconds, stopping to scrape sides as necessary, until smooth.

2) Pour into 2 glasses. Serve immediately.

41. Spinach Blueberry Pomegranate Smoothies

Ingridients:

✓ 1 cup fat-free (skim) milk

✓ 1/3 cup cooked green frozen spinach, squeezed to drain

✓ Juice of 1 medium lime (2 to 3 tablespoons)

✓ 1 pouch (7.6 oz) smoothie blueberry pomegranate

Instructions:

1) In blender, place all ingredients. Cover; blend on high speed 1 minute to 1 minute 30 seconds, stopping to scrape sides as necessary, until smooth.

2) Pour into 2 glasses. Serve immediately.

42. Mixed Berry Cheesecake Smoothie Parfaits

Ingridients:

√ 3/4 cup fat-free (skim) milk

√ 1/4 cup strawberry cream cheese

√ 1 pouch (4.5 oz) smoothie greek mixed berry

√ 1 cup chopped fresh strawberries

√ 2 oats 'n dark chocolate crunchy granola bars (1 pouch from 8.94-oz box), coarsely crushed

√ Whipped cream topping in aerosol can, if desired

Instructions:

1) In blender, place milk, cream cheese and contents of smoothie pouch. Cover; blend on high speed 1 minute to 1 minute 30 seconds, stopping to scrape sides as necessary, until smooth.

2) Pour about 1/2 cup mixture in each of 2 glasses. Top each with about 1/4 cup strawberries and 1 heaping tablespoonful crushed granola bar. Repeat. Top with whipped topping. Serve immediately.

43. Strawberry Banana Nut Oatmeal Smoothies

Ingridients:

✓ 1 cup fat-free (skim) milk

✓ 1 packet regular-flavor instant oatmeal

✓ 1/4 cup walnuts

✓ 1 pouch (7.6 oz) smoothie strawberry banana

Instructions:

1) In blender, place all ingredients. Cover; blend on high speed 1 minute to 1 minute 30 seconds, stopping to scrape sides as necessary, until smooth.

2) Pour into 2 glasses. Serve immediately.

44. Peanutty Chocolate Banana Smoothies

Ingridients:

✓ 1 cup fat-free (skim) milk

✓ 1/4 cup cocktail peanuts

✓ 3 tablespoons peanut butter

✓ 1 pouch (7.6 oz) smoothie chocolate banana

Instructions:

1) In blender, place all ingredients. Cover; blend on high speed 1 minute to 1 minute 30 seconds, stopping to scrape sides as necessary, until smooth.

2) Pour into 2 glasses. Serve immediately.

45. Fresh Strawberry Smoothies

Ingridients:

√ 1 pint (2 cups) fresh strawberries

√ 1 cup milk

√ 2 containers (6 oz each) strawberry low-fat yogurt

Instructions:

1) Place the strawberries in a strainer and rinse under cold running water. Gently pat dry with paper towels. Reserve 4 strawberries for the garnish. Cut out the hull, or "cap," from the remaining strawberries with the point of a paring knife.

2) In a blender or food processor, place the strawberries, milk and yogurt.

3) Cover; blend on high speed about 30 seconds or until smooth. Pour into glasses. Garnish each with a strawberry.

46. North Pole Strawberry Smoothie

Ingridients:

√ 1 package (10 ounces) frozen strawberries in syrup, partially thawed and undrained

√ 1/4 cup water

√ 2 cups vanilla frozen yogurt

√ 2 tablespoons vanilla reduced-fat yogurt

√ 1 strawberry-flavored or peppermint candy cane, about 6 inches long, finely crushed

√ Betty Crocker green decorating gel

Instructions:

1) Place strawberries and water in blender. Cover and blend on medium-high speed until slushy. Blend on medium speed until smooth. Transfer to 2-cup measure.

2) Wash and dry blender. Place frozen yogurt and reduced-fat yogurt in blender. Cover and blend on medium speed until smooth.

3) Place crushed candy cane on small plate. Pipe decorating gel around rim of two 12-ounce glasses. Dip rims into crushed candy.

4) Carefully pour yogurt mixture and strawberries at the same time into glasses, creating a half-and-half design. Serve with large drinking straws if desired.

47. Lucky Charms Raspberry Smoothie

Ingridients:

✓ 1 container (6 oz) raspberry or strawberry yogurt

✓ 3/4 cup cereal

✓ 1/2 cup fresh or frozen raspberries

✓ 1 cup fat free (skim) milk

✓ 1/2 banana, sliced

Instructions:

1) In blender, place ingredients. Cover; blend on high speed about 30 seconds or until smooth, stopping blender once to scrape sides.

2) Pour into 2 glasses. Serve immediately.

48. Creamy Strawberry Rhubarb Smoothies

Ingridients:

√ 1 cup frozen chopped rhubarb

√ 1 cup frozen strawberries

√ 1 container (6 oz) greek honey vanilla yogurt

√ 2 tablespoons agave nectar

√ 1 cup cranberry-raspberry juice

Instructions:

1) In blender, place all ingredients. Cover; blend with on-and-off pulses until pureed. Pour into 2 drinking glasses. Serve immediately.

49. Apple Turnover Smoothies

Ingridients:

✓ 2 containers (6 oz each) apple turnover yogurt

✓ 1/2 cup unsweetened applesauce

✓ 1 cup chopped apple

✓ Apple pie spice

✓ Apple slices

Instructions:

1) In blender, place yogurt, applesauce and chopped apple. Cover; blend on medium speed until smooth.

2) Pour into 2 glasses; top with apple pie spice and apple slice.

50. Key Lime-Banana Smoothie

Ingridients:

✓ 1 container (6 oz) lime pie yogurt

✓ 1 ripe banana, sliced

✓ 1/2 cup milk

✓ 1 tablespoon lime juice

✓ 1/4 teaspoon dry lemon lime-flavored soft drink mix (from 0.13-oz package)

✓ 1 cup vanilla frozen yogurt

Instructions:

1) Place all ingredients except frozen yogurt in blender. Cover; blend on high speed until smooth.

2) Add frozen yogurt. Cover; blend until smooth.

51. Peach-Banana Smoothie

Ingridients:

✓ 1 medium banana, cut up

✓ 1 ripe medium peach, pitted, sliced

✓ 1 (6-oz.) container low-fat peach yogurt

✓ 1/4 cup orange juice

✓ 1 teaspoon honey

✓ 1 cup small ice cubes

Instructions:

1) Combine all ingredients in blender container; blend 1 to 2 minutes or until smooth and frothy.

52. Citrus-Peach Smoothie

Ingridients:

✓ *1 container (8 ounces) lemon fat-free yogurt*

✓ *1 cup unsweetened frozen, fresh or canned (drained) sliced peaches*

✓ *3/4 cup calcium-fortified orange juice*

✓ *3 tablespoons blueberries, if desired*

Instructions:

1) Place yogurt, peaches and orange juice in blender. Cover and blend on high speed about 30 seconds or until smooth.

2) Pour mixture into glasses. Garnish with blueberries.

53. Granola Berry-Banana Smoothies

Ingridients:

√ 2 containers (6 oz each) strawberry, mixed berry or red raspberry yogurt

√ 1/2 cup milk

√ 1/2 cup fresh strawberry halves or raspberries

√ 1 banana, sliced

√ 2 pouches (1.5 oz each) oats 'n honey crunchy granola bars (4 bars)

Instructions:

1) In blender, place yogurt, milk, strawberry halves and banana slices. Break up 3 granola bars; add to blender. Cover and blend on high speed 10 sec. Scrape sides.

2) Cover and blend about 20 sec longer or until smooth.

3) Pour into 2 glasses. Crumble remaining bar; sprinkle in each glass. Serve immediately.

54. Orange-Carrot-Banana Smoothies

Ingridients:

✓ 1 1/2 cups creamy vanilla yogurt (from 2-lb container)

✓ 1 cup chopped fresh pineapple

✓ 3/4 cup orange juice

✓ 2/3 cup purchased carrot juice

✓ 1 medium banana, cut into pieces

Instructions:

1) In blender, place all ingredients. Cover; blend on high speed 1 to 2 minutes until smooth. Serve immediately.

55. Strawberry-Orange Smoothies

Ingridients:

✓ 2 cups creamy vanilla yogurt

✓ 1 bag (10 oz) frozen organic strawberries

✓ 2 tablespoons orange juice

✓ 1 tablespoon honey

Instructions:

1) In blender, place ingredients. Cover; blend on medium speed until smooth. Add more honey to taste if desired.

2) Pour into 3 glasses. Serve immediately.

56. Honey Nut-Peach Smoothies

Ingridients:

✓ 1 1/3 cups creamy harvest peach or creamy vanilla yogurt (from 2-lb container)

✓ 1 1/2 cups honey nut cereal

✓ 1 can (15 oz) sliced peaches in juice, drained

✓ 1 cup milk

✓ 1 banana, sliced

✓ 1/8 teaspoon ground cinnamon, if desired

Instructions:

1) In blender, place ingredients. Cover; blend on high speed 10 seconds. Scrape down sides of blender. Cover; blend about 20 seconds longer or until smooth.

2) Pour into 4 glasses. Serve immediately.

57. Cocoa-Peanut Butter-Banana Smoothies

Ingridients:

√ 1 1/2 cups creamy vanilla yogurt (from 2 lb container)

√ 1 cup chocolate milk

√ 1/4 cup creamy peanut butter

√ 2 small bananas, sliced

√ 3 to 5 ice cubes

√ 1 cup Cocoa Puffs cereal, coarsely crushed

Instructions:

1) Place all ingredients except cereal in blender. Cover; blend on high speed about 30 seconds or until smooth.

2) Pour into 4 glasses. Sprinkle with cereal. Serve immediately.

58. Papaya-Colada Smoothies

Ingridients:

✓ 1 papaya

✓ 1 (8-oz.) can crushed pineapple in unsweetened juice, undrained

✓ 1 pint (2 cups) nonfat vanilla frozen yogurt

✓ 1/2 cup orange juice

✓ 3/4 teaspoon coconut extract

Instructions:

1) Cut papaya in half; scoop out and discard seeds. Scoop flesh from skin into food processor bowl with metal blade.

2) Add pineapple with juice; process until smooth. Add frozen yogurt, orange juice and extract; process until smooth.

59. Easy Being Green Smoothies

Ingridients:

✓ 1 box (9 oz) green frozen chopped spinach

✓ 1 container (6 oz) lime pie yogurt

✓ 2 medium kiwifruit, peeled, quartered

✓ 1/2 cup ice cubes

✓ 1/3 cup apple juice

Instructions:

1) Microwave spinach as directed on box. Rinse with cold water until cooled. Drain, squeezing out as much liquid as possible.

2) In blender, place 1/3 cup of the cooked spinach and all remaining ingredients. (Cover and refrigerate remaining spinach for another use.) Cover; blend on high speed about 30 seconds or until smooth.

3) Pour into 2 glasses. Serve immediately.

60. Berry Cheesecake Smoothies

Ingridients:

✓ 1 bag (12 oz) frozen mixed berries

✓ 2 cups skim milk

✓ 2/3 cup cream cheese flavored frosting

✓ 1/4 cup triple berry preserves

✓ 1 1/3 cups whipped cream topping (from aerosol can)

✓ 1 teaspoon graham cracker crumbs

Instructions:

1) Reserve 12 frozen blueberries from the mixed berries for garnish. In blender, place remaining mixed berries, milk, frosting and preserves. Cover; blend on medium-high speed 30 seconds, stopping once to scrape sides, until smooth.

2) Pour into glasses. Top with whipped cream topping, graham cracker crumbs and reserved frozen blueberries.

61. Chocolate Pumpkin Mudslide

Ingridients:

√ 1/4 cup Irish cream liqueur

√ 1/4 cup coffee-flavored liqueur

√ 1/4 cup vodka

√ 3 cups vanilla ice cream

√ 1 cup canned pumpkin (not pumpkin pie mix)

√ 1 teaspoon pumpkin pie spice

√ 8 teaspoons chocolate-flavor syrup

√ Whipped cream topping (from aerosol can), if desired

√ Additional pumpkin pie spice, if desired

Instructions:

1) In blender, place liqueurs, vodka, ice cream, pumpkin and 1 teaspoon pumpkin pie spice. Cover; blend on high speed until smooth.

2) Into each of 4 cocktail glasses, drizzle 2 teaspoons chocolate syrup. Pour ice cream mixture evenly into glasses. Garnish with whipped cream topping and additional pumpkin pie spice. Serve immediately.

62. Freeze-Ahead Tropical Smoothies

Ingridients:

√ 3 bags (16 oz each) frozen tropical fruit

√ 1 container (2 lb) creamy vanilla yogurt

√ 2 cans (12 oz) frozen orange juice concentrate, thawed

Instructions:

1) Divide frozen fruit evenly among 8 quart-size resealable freezer plastic bags. Add 1/2 cup yogurt and 1/4 cup orange juice concentrate to each bag. (Save remaining orange juice concentrate for another use.) Seal bags; freeze up to 3 months.

2) To prepare smoothie, place bag(s) in refrigerator and thaw just until fruit mixture can be removed from bag. In blender, place contents of 1 bag and 1 cup cold water. Cover; blend on high speed about 30 seconds or until smooth. Pour into 3 glasses. Serve immediately.

63. Oatmeal Cookie Smoothie

Ingridients:

✓ 1/4 cup old-fashioned oats

✓ 1 frozen (peeled) banana

✓ 1 cup unsweetened almond milk

✓ 1-2 Tbsp honey (to taste)

✓ 1/2 tsp ground cinnamon

✓ 1/2 tsp vanilla extract

✓ 1/4 tsp ground ginger

✓ Pinch of nutmeg

✓ Pinch of salt

✓ Optional: 1/4 cup raisins

Instructions:

1) Add oats to blender, and pulse until finely ground. Add remaining ingredients and pulse until blended and smooth. Serve immediately.

64. White Smoothie

Ingridients:

✓ 2 apples, cored

✓ 2 bananas, peeled and frozen

✓ 1 Tbsp peanut butter

✓ 1/2 cup milk or coconut milk

✓ 1/2 cup ice (if needed)

Instructions:

1) Combine all ingredients in a blender and mix until smooth and well-combined.

65. Avocado And Coconut Water Smoothies

Ingridients:

√ 2 1/4 cups coconut water, chilled

√ 2 ripe avocados, pitted, peeled and cut into pieces

√ 3 tablespoons agave nectar

√ 2 teaspoons fresh lime juice

Instructions:

1) Fill 14-cube ice-cube tray with 2 cups of the cold coconut water. Freeze until solid.

2) In blender, place avocado, coconut water ice cubes, remaining 1/4 cup cold coconut water, agave nectar and lime juice. Cover; blend with on-and-off pulses until creamy and smooth.

3) Pour into drinking glasses. Serve immediately.

66. Peanut Butter And Berry Smoothies

Ingridients:

✓ 1 cup light vanilla soymilk

✓ 2 tablespoons creamy peanut butter

✓ 1 bag (7.6 oz) smoothie strawberry banana

Instructions:

1) In blender, place soy milk, peanut butter and contents of Yoplait Frozen Smoothie bag. Cover; blend on high speed 1 minute to 1 minute 30 seconds, stopping blender to scrape down sides as necessary, until smooth. Pour into glasses.

67. Strawberry Cheesecake Shakes

Ingridients:

√ 2 cups strawberry ice cream, slightly softened

√ 2 tablespoon strawberry-flavored or regular milk

√ 6 ounces cream cheese, softened

√ 1 tablespoon powdered sugar

√ 1/12 piece cooled unfrosted white cake, cut into chunks (from 13x9-inch pan)

√ Graham cracker crumbs, if desired

√ Sliced fresh strawberries, if desired

Instructions:

1) In blender, place ice cream and milk. Cover and blend on high speed until smooth and creamy. Add cream cheese, powdered sugar and cake chunks; cover and blend until smooth, stopping blender to scrape down sides if necessary.

2) Pour into 2 glasses; top with graham cracker crumbs and sliced strawberries. Serve immediately.

68. Red Smoothie

Ingridients:

✓ 2 cups frozen strawberries

✓ 1 mango, peeled and cored

✓ 1/2 cup cranberry juice (or other juice)

✓ 1/2 cup ice (if needed)

Instructions:

1) Combine all ingredients in a blender and mix until smooth and well-combined.

69. Raspberry-Banana Yogurt Smoothies

Ingridients:

✓ 1 container (6 oz) vanilla yogurt

✓ 1 1/2 cups soymilk

✓ 1 cup unsweetened frozen or fresh raspberries

✓ 1 medium banana, sliced (1 cup)

Instructions:

1) Place ingredients in blender or food processor. Cover; blend on high speed about 30 seconds or until smooth.

2) Pour into 2 glasses. Serve immediately.

70. Yellow Smoothie

Ingridients:

✓ 2 cups fresh pineapple, cut into large pieces

✓ 1 banana

✓ 1/2 cup coconut milk (I used "light" coconut milk)

✓ 1/2 cup ice

Instructions:

1) Combine all ingredients in a blender and mix until smooth and well-combined.

71. Cinnamon Pear Oatmeal Breakfast Smoothie

Ingridients:

✓ 1/2 cup pear, shredded (73 grams)

✓ 1/4 cup rolled oats (I used Gluten Free)

✓ 1/2 tsp. cinnamon

✓ 1/4 tsp. stevia (to taste)

✓ 1/2 cup greek yogurt, plain 0% fat

✓ 3/4 cup non-fat milk or coconut milk, unsweetened from carton

Instructions:

1) Place all ingredients in a blender and process until smooth. If the smoothie is to thick, add a pinch more milk.

72. Strawberry Oatmeal Smoothie Bowl

Ingridients:

✓ 1/3 cup rolled oats

✓ 1 tsp chia seeds

✓ 1/2 cup Wallaby Strawberry Keifer

✓ 1/2 cup non-fat milk or milk of your choice

✓ 1 cup strawberries, frozen

Instructions:

1) The night before, in a bowl add rolled oats, chia seeds and Strawberry Keifer. Mix well, cover and refrigerate over night.

2) In the morning, add the rolled oats mixture in a blender and add milk and frozen strawberries and process until smooth.

3) Pour into a bowl and enjoy! Top with peanut butter, nuts or whatever you desire.

73. Raspberry-Peach Iced Tea Smoothies

Ingridients:

✓ 1 cup frozen whole raspberries without syrup (about 4 1/2 oz)

✓ 3/4 cup milk

✓ 2 tablespoons sugar-free low-calorie peach iced tea mix

✓ 1 container (6 oz) white chocolate raspberry yogurt

✓ 1 bag (16 oz) frozen sliced peaches without syrup, 2 slices reserved and thawed

Instructions:

1) In blender container, cover and blend raspberries, milk, tea mix and yogurt on high speed until smooth.

2) Add half of the peach slices; cover and blend on high speed until smooth. Add remaining peaches; cover and blend until smooth. Pour into glasses.

3) Cut reserved thawed peach slices in half crosswise. Garnish glasses with peach pieces.

74. Cheerios Smoothies

Ingridients:

√ 1 cup milk

√ 1 cup Cheerios cereal

√ 1 ripe banana, cut into chunks

√ 1 cup ice

√ Banana slices, if desired

Instructions:

1) In blender, place milk, cereal, banana chunks and ice. Cover; blend on high speed about 30 seconds or until smooth.

2) Pour into 2 glasses. Garnish with banana slices. Serve immediately.

75. Green Apple Avocado Green Smoothie

Ingridients:

✓ 1/2 avocado

✓ 2 small green apples

✓ 1/4 cup of light yogurt

✓ 1 cup of milk

✓ 2 tbs honey

✓ 2-3 ice cubes

Instructions:

1) Peeling the apples is up to you. It will alter the texture of the smoothie if you choose to leave the skin on but it will also keep most of the vitamins in the smoothie. If you don't mind the texture, I recommend keeping the skin and just coring the apples.

2) Combine the chopped, cored apples, cut avocado, yogurt, milk, honey and ice in the blender.

3) Pulse very well until nice and smooth.

4) Serve immediately.

76. Grapefruit-Gin Cocktail Shakes

Ingridients:

√ 1 pint raspberry sorbet

√ 1/3 cup pink grapefruit juice, chilled

√ 1 pint vanilla ice cream

√ 1/4 cup gin or pink grapefruit juice

√ Lemon Slices

Instructions:

1) In a blender combine sorbet and 1/3 cup grapefruit juice;
cover and blend until smooth. Blend in ice cream and gin. If
necessary, blend in additional juice. Divide among four tall
glasses. Garnish with lemon slices. Makes 4 servings.

77. Blueberry Pie Milkshake

Ingridients:

✓ 1 graham cracker, split in half

✓ 2 tbsp marshmallow cream ice cream topping

✓ 1/2 cup milk

✓ 2 cups chocolate ice cream

Instructions:

1) In blender or food processor, place all ingredients. Cover; blend on high speed 20 to 30 seconds or until smooth.

2) Pour into 2 glasses. Serve immediately.

78. Salted Caramel Brownie Milkshake

Ingridients:

✓ 1/2 cup milk

✓ 3 scoops vanilla ice cream

✓ 1 Salted Caramel Skillet Brownie

✓ 3 tablespoons Salted Caramel Sauce

✓ Whipped cream, for serving, optional

✓ Extra salted caramel sauce and brownie pieces for decorating, optional

Instructions:

1) In a blender, combine the milk, ice cream, brownie, and salted caramel sauce. Blend until smooth. Pour into glass and top with whipped cream, if using. Garnish with extra salted caramel sauce and brownie chunks, if desired. Serve immediately.

79. Red Velvet Cake Milkshake

Ingridients:

✓ 1 red velvet cake cupcake

✓ ½ cup milk

✓ 2 scoops vanilla ice cream

Instructions:

1) Add milk and vanilla ice cream to blender and blend just until combined. Break cupcake into large chunks and gently stir into milkshake.

2) Serve immediately.

80. Buttercrunch Milkshakes for Grown Ups

Ingridients:

√ 1 pint chocolate ice cream

√ 1/4 cup buttershots schnapps

√ 3/4 cup amaretto liqueur

√ 1/3 cup buttercrunch candy, crushed

√ 2 tablespoons whipped cream

Instructions:

1) Put ice cream, buttershots, amaretto, and buttercrunch (leave a bit behind for garnish) in a blender.

2) Blend until smooth. Pour into 2 glasses and garnish with whipped cream and reserved buttercrunch.

81. Strawberry Milkshake

Ingridients:

✓ ½ cup milk

✓ 2 scoops vanilla ice cream

✓ ¼ cup strawberry syrup

Instructions:

1) Add all ingredients to blender and blend just until all ingredients are combined, but not until the fruit has been completely pureed.

82. S'mores Milkshakes

Ingridients:

✓ 1 graham cracker, split in half

✓ 2 tbsp marshmallow cream ice cream topping

✓ 1/2 cup milk

✓ 2 cups chocolate ice cream

Instructions:

1) Combine the chocolate ice cream and milk in a blender. Whirl until smooth. Divide between two glasses.

2) Drizzle the marshmallow cream into each glass. Top with 1/2 of the graham cracker

3) Enjoy immediately.

83. Black-Bottomed Cherry Shakes

Ingridients:

✓ 3 cups cherry ice cream

✓ 1/4 cup dark chocolate shavings, if desired

✓ 1 to 2 cups milk

✓ 1/2 cup hot fudge topping

✓ 2/3 cup whipped topping

✓ 2 cherries

Instructions:

1) In blender, combine ice cream, chocolate shavings and milk; blend until smooth.

2) Into each of 2 large drinking glasses, spoon 1/4 cup of the hot fudge topping. Add milkshake to each glass. Spoon whipped topping on top of each and top with a cherry.

84. DIY Shamrock Shakes

Ingridients:

√ 3 cups vanilla ice cream

√ 1 cup milk

√ 1/2 teaspoon mint extract

√ GEL green food coloring or PASTE food coloring recommended

√ 2 cups 2 whipped cream

√ Sprinkles

Instructions:

1) Combine the ice cream, milk, mint extract and food coloring in a blender and pulse until combined. Add more green food coloring as desired.

2) Transfer the shakes to serving glasses, then top with whipped cream and sprinkles. Serve immediately.

85. Avocado Milkshake

Ingridients:

✓ 1 Ripe Avocado

✓ 1 1/2 Cups Vanilla Ice Cream

✓ 1/2 Cup Milk

✓ 2/3 Cups Heavy Whipping Cream (topping)

✓ 1 Lemon Zest only (topping)

✓ 1 Tablespoon Sugar (topping)

✓ 1/2 Teaspoon Vanilla Extract (topping)

✓ 2 Marascino Cherries (topping)

Instructions:

1) For the whipped cream, add cold heavy cream to a cold bowl (preferably stainless steel). Add sugar and vanilla. Whisk until it forms stiff peaks. Fold in lemon zest. Refrigerate until needed.

2) Cut avocado in half and remove seed with a knife (be careful).

3) Add ice cream, milk, and avocado to a blender. Blend until smooth!

4) Split avocado shake between two glasses and top with lots of lemon whipped cream.

5) Garnish with a cherry!

86. Layered Chocolate Fro-Yo Milkshake

Ingridients:

√ 2 pints Yoplait Greek Vanilla Frozen Yogurt

√ 4 tablespoons Betty Crocker Hershey's Special Dark Chocolate Frosting

√ 2 tablespoons Betty Crocker Hershey's Milk Chocolate Frosting

√ 1/2 cup whipped cream

√ 4 tablespoons chocolate syrup

√ 2 tablespoons chocolate chunks

Instructions:

1) In a blender, blend 1 1/2 cups frozen yogurt with Hershey's Special Dark frosting. Spoon into the bottom of four milkshake glasses. Place in freezer while prepping the next step.

2) Add 1 1/2 cups yogurt to the blender, and place 2 tablespoons Milk Chocolate frosting in it. Blend until smooth. Pour slowly over the back of a spoon on top of dark chocolate layer. Return to freezer.

3) Place 1 1/2 cups frozen yogurt into the blender (without cleaning the blender, to retain a bit of that chocolate flavor). Blend until smooth. Spoon on top of the milkshakes.

4) Top with whipped cream, drizzle with chocolate syrup. Sprinkle with chopped chocolate.

87. Raw Spiced Chocolate Milkshake

Ingridients:

✓ 2 cups almond milk (homemade or storebought)

✓ 2 Tbsp agave nectar or honey

✓ 3 frozen bananas

✓ 1 Tbsp raw cacao powder

✓ 1 tsp ground cinnamon

✓ Pinch of salt

✓ 1/4 tsp cayenne pepper powder (add more or less to taste)

✓ 1/4 tsp chili powder

Instructions:

1) Combine all ingredients in a blender until combined. Serve immediately, or pop the mixture in the freezer for an hour to give it an extra chill.

2) Serve topped with shaved cacao nibs or a sprinkle of cinnamon if desired.

88. Peach Pie Milkshake

Ingridients:

√ 1/2 package Pillsbury Refrigerated Pie
Crust (1 9-inch crust)

√ 1 1/4 cups frozen sliced peaches, thawed
(or use fresh when in season)

√ 1 tsp. cornstarch

√ 1/2 tsp. lemon juice

√ 1/2 tsp. ground cinnamon

√ 2 TBSP granulated sugar

√ 8 scoops vanilla bean ice cream

√ Thin milk to

√ As whipped cream garnish

Instructions:

To make the Hand Pies:

1) In a medium size bowl add diced peaches, cinnamon, lemon juice, sugar, and cornstarch.

2) Mix until all the ingredients are fully incorporated and a syrup forms.

3) Roll out the prepared crust.

4) Place three heaping spoonful's of peach filling into the lower half of the pie crust, leaving a space between each spoonful so as to get three hand pies.

5) Fold over the top half of the pie crust. Cut into three parts.

6) Crimp the edges with a fork and seal the pie filling into the crust. Some filling (mostly juices) will come out during baking, that's okay.

7) Place on to a greased baking sheet. Bake at 400F for 14-16 minutes.

8) Remove from oven and let cool.

To Make the Shake:

1) To a blender add 4 scoops of Vanilla Bean Ice Cream and one hand pie. Using milk to thin. Blend the shake to desired consistency. Repeat and make a second milkshake.

2) Top milkshake with whipped cream and half of the third hand pie. Use the other half of the hand pie for the second shake.

89. Pumpkin Pie Milkshakes

Ingridients:

Bourbon whipped cream

- √ 1/2 cup heavy cream
- √ 1 tablespoon bourbon
- √ 2 tablespoons sugar
- √ 1/2 teaspoon vanilla extract

Milkshakes

- √ 2 cups vanilla ice cream
- √ 1/2 cup pumpkin puree
- √ 1/3 cup milk
- √ 1 tablespoon bourbon
- √ 1/2 teaspoon cinnamon
- √ 1/4 teaspoon nutmeg

Instructions:

1) For whipped cream, whisk together cream, bourbon, sugar, and vanilla in a cold metal bowl until it holds stiff peaks. Store in the fridge until needed.

2) For milkshake, combine ice cream, pumpkin, milk, bourbon, and spices in a blender and blend until smooth.

3) Pour milk shake between two cups, top with bourbon; whipped cream, and sprinkle with ground cinnamon.

90. Angel Food Cake Shakes

Ingridients:

✓ 2 cups vanilla fat-free frozen yogurt, slightly softened

✓ 1/4 cup fat-free (skim) milk

✓ 1/12 cooled slice angel food cake, torn into pieces (from 12-inch cake)

✓ Fat-free whipped topping, thawed, if desired

✓ Fresh berries, if desired

✓ Reduced-calorie chocolate-flavor syrup, if desired

Instructions:

1) In blender, place yogurt and milk. Cover and blend on high speed until smooth and creamy. Add cake pieces; cover and blend until smooth, stopping blender to scrape down sides if necessary.

2) Pour into 2 glasses; top with whipped topping and berries. Drizzle with chocolate syrup. Serve immediately.   97

91. Snickerdoodle Shakes

Ingridients:

√ 2 cups vanilla ice cream, slightly softened

√ 1/3 cup milk

√ 3/4 teaspoon ground cinnamon

√ 2 cooled sugar or snickerdoodle cookies (3-inch), quartered

√ Sweetened whipped cream, if desired

√ Additional sugar or snickerdoodle cookies, coarsely crumbled, if desired

√ Ground cinnamon, if desired

Instructions:

1) In blender, place ice cream, milk and cinnamon. Cover and blend on high speed until smooth and creamy. Add cookie pieces; cover and blend until smooth, stopping blender to scrape down sides if necessary.

2) Pour into 2 glasses; top with sweetened whipped cream; sprinkle with crumbled cookies and cinnamon. Serve immediately.

92. Strawberry coconut "milk"shake

Ingridients:

✓ 1 (10 oz.) bag frozen strawberries (hulled)

✓ 1 1/2 cups coconut milk, either homemade or storebought

Instructions:

1) Place ingredients in a blender, and blend on high speed until smooth.

93. Dulce De Leche Shakes

Ingridients:

✓ 2 cups vanilla ice cream, slightly softened

✓ 1/4 cup dulce de leche (caramelized sweetened condensed milk from 13.4 oz can)

✓ 2 tablespoons milk

✓ 1/12 piece cooled unfrosted white cake, cut into chunks (from 13x9-inch pan)

✓ Sweetened whipped cream, if desired

✓ Caramel topping, if desired

Instructions:

1) In blender, place ice cream, dulce de leche and milk. Cover and blend on high speed until smooth and creamy. Add cake chunks; cover and blend until smooth, stopping blender to scrape down sides if necessary.

2) Pour into 2 glasses; top with sweetened whipped cream and drizzle with caramel. Serve immediately.

94. Iced Mint Mocha

Ingridients:

✓ 4 cups cold milk

✓ 10 red-striped mint candies, roughly chopped

✓ 2 tablespoons instant coffee granules

✓ ½ cup chocolate syrup

✓ 4 cups ice cubes

✓ 4 fresh mint sprigs for garnish

Instructions:

1) Place all of the ingredients, except for the mint sprigs and ice, in a blender and puree until smooth.

2) Evenly divide the ice cubes among 4 large glasses, pour the mint mocha over the ice.

3) Garnish each with a mint sprig, then serve.

95. Skinny Piña Colada Float

Ingridients:

✓ 1 to 2 Sparkling Ice Coconut Pineapple Water bottles

✓ 4 frozen yogurt bars, 2 scoops per mug

Instructions:

1) Cool the mugs that you will be using for the floats. (in the fridge for about 30+ minutes)

2) Cut the frozen yogurt pops off the stick and cut them into chunks. (If using frozen yogurt just scoop two scoops per mug.)

3) Slowly, aiming to the side, pour in the sparkling water until full.

96. Frappuccino Recipe

Ingridients:

✓ 2 cups crushed ice

✓ 1 cup espresso (or very strong coffee)

✓ ¾ cup half and half, or your preferred milk, soy, or almond

✓ 2 tablespoons granulated sugar, or sugar substitute

✓ Whipped cream (optional)

✓ Chocolate syrup (optional)

Instructions:

1) Blend together crushed ice, espresso, half and half, and sugar until well-blended. Pour into glass and top with whipped cream and a drizzle of chocolate syrup, if desired.

2) Serve immediately.

97. Pumpkin Pie Milkshake

Ingridients:

√ 1/2 cup pure pumpkin (not pumpkin pie filling)

√ 1 cup vanilla ice cream

√ 3/4 cup milk

√ 3/4 tsp pumpkin pie spice

√ 2 tsp caramel ice cream topping

√ 5 vanilla wafers, crushed

Instructions:

1) Combine pumpkin, ice cream, milk and spice in a blender.

2) Blend until smooth.

3) Dip a glass into a bowl with the caramel.

4) Next dip the glass into the crushed wafers.

5) Pour milkshake in carefully and top with additional pumpkin pie spice if desired.

98. Bacon Milkshakes

Ingridients:

√ 3 tablespoons real maple syrup

√ 2 slices bacon, cooked

√ 2 cups vanilla ice cream

√ 1/2 cup milk

Instructions:

1) In 1-quart saucepan, heat syrup and 1 slice of the bacon over medium heat 2 to 3 minutes. Remove from heat; set aside to infuse bacon flavor into syrup.

2) In blender, place ice cream and milk. Cover; blend on medium speed until combined.

3) Remove bacon from syrup; discard bacon. Add syrup to milk mixture; blend on low speed to combine.

4) Divide milkshake evenly between 2 glasses. Crumble remaining slice of cooked bacon; sprinkle over tops of milkshakes.

99. Berry Pie Shakes

Ingridients:

√ 2 cups vanilla ice cream, slightly softened

√ 2 tablespoons milk

√ 1/8 slice cold baked blueberry, cherry or raspberry pie, cut into chunks (from 9-inch pie)

√ Sweetened whipped cream, if desired

√ Fresh blueberries, pitted bing cherries or raspberries, if desired

Instructions:

1) In blender, place ice cream and milk. Cover and blend on high speed until smooth and creamy. Add pie chunks; cover and blend until smooth, stopping blender to scrape down sides if necessary.

2) Pour into 2 glasses; top with sweetened whipped cream and garnish with berries. Serve immediately.

100. Lemon Meringue Pie Shakes

Ingridients:

√ 2 cups vanilla ice cream, slightly softened

√ 1/4 cup milk

√ 1 teaspoon sugar-free lemonade flavor drink mix (from 2.1-oz container)

√ 1 slice cold lemon meringue pie, cut into chunks (from 9-inch pie)

√ Crushed lemon drops, if desired

Instructions:

1) In blender, place ice cream, milk and lemonade mix. Cover and blend on high speed until smooth and creamy. Add pie chunks; cover and blend until smooth, stopping blender to scrape down sides if necessary.

2) Pour into 2 glasses; sprinkle with crushed lemon drops. Serve immediately.

Made in the USA
Monee, IL
26 November 2020